Pull N[...]

A revolution in selling for people who hate it!!

By

Lisa Ansell

Contents

This Book is very simple

1. Everyone needs this book
2. Introduction - don't skip this! Understanding the motivation of your inspiration is essential!
3. Sales AND Marketing- the "build it and they will come" mythology
4. Where does it all go wrong?
5. Evolution - My Inspiration
6. The 'Pull not push' strategy
7. Design your own 'Pull not push' strategies
8. Case studies and templates - Why?
   Case study 1 – Inventory Franchisee
   Case study 2 – Age advisory company
9. Identifying your selling process
10. My Parting gifts- The elements of success
11. About the Author
12. What next

This book is VERY simple….

All the methods in this book are simple…

The Greatest thing is that they are PROVEN to WORK

How do I know this?

These methods have been tried and tested for over 20 years of hard graft; as a salesperson, as a business owner, being at the head of national and international companies, and as a specialist business consultant.

I believe I am the world's most reluctant salesperson.

The reason got into sales was that I needed a way to make money, plain and simple... I am a creative, an enthusiastic one but I absolutely cannot stand selling.

When I say I hate selling, I mean I cannot bear the arrogant, one-upmanship, trickery, Americanised, overly macho rubbish that comes with it... I do love achievement, recognition and excellence.

What I hate is the concept that it is somehow adversarial or that it's a contest of wits or that people can be outsmarted into buying somehow. Certainly in both the business to business and the business to consumer markets, I have come across this belief.

As a consumer, I cannot bear the clumsy, arrogant, deaf sales pitches barked down the phone by underwhelming telesales people, interrupting your day. I also understand the proactive approaches by salespeople in our day to day lives, can be irritating when we spend so much time lost in our busy worlds and doing our very best to be very British and deferring interaction when going about our business.

The obvious recent example is the PPI compensation business... We all love a call from these bad boys! I find the most annoying calls are the ones they do not even get a real person to make the call and you get a recorded message!! COME ON!! Rant over...

"PPI....Accident lately? Blah....blah"

It is understandable that we do have an aversion to being seen as a sales person or have an internal resistance to making sales calls.

My solution is to not make sales calls….but when is a selling call not a sales call? And how have I survived this world of hard selling?

I did it my way…. I took all of the clever strategies, all of the positive, embedded Neuro-linguistic programming….. and I just asked and listened….

Guess what? It worked!

When I decided to publish this gem of a book, I consulted with a number of people who tried to persuade me that blogs and Ebooks were the way forward, the path to success. Now I am a lover of all things new and exciting, accessible and most importantly successful. But, I have always had and still have a strong belief that this needed to be a workbook…. a pocketed companion…. a familiar and handy constant guide, something people would ACTUALLY USE!

With EBooks you cannot scribble comments, observations, how to use or draw inspired, enlightening and amusing doodles!

I want you to absorb this guide, own it, utilise it as you need, add your own insights, knowledge and light bulb moments.

This is why this book is formatted the way it is. Every other page is this book is a blank page. This page is FOR YOU, use it as you will, but use it well.

We'd love see your meaningful insights as you fill in these pages. Scan, email and share with us.

THIS BOOK NEEDS YOU!

For those sharp-eyed cynics who are looking for the catch….. Here it is! By using this book in the way it's intended, is to openly accept this methodology. The first step is to imbed these methods it into the fabric of your business. And by you contributing to its pages, you are the first example of Pull NOT Push practices. Inviting you to own the spaces in this book is an important example of "give to get" in action.

Our human brains are brilliantly fascinating, highly clumsy and cack-handed organs. They have interesting foibles that regularly try, and succeed in, tripping us up.

One of these foibles is that to be able to get really important stuff to stick (some of us resemble Teflon more than others), it is believed that we have to process and experience information in three different ways, these could be reading, repeating or writing. So, interacting with this book in this way, molding the theories and thoughts into your own words or experience/s, will bring about the sticky effect that's required to absorb this wisdom with the ability to utilise to your greatest benefit.

Read, absorb, adapt and adopt.... Practice what you read and if you have any questions, you can always email me!

pullnotpushrevolution@gmail.com. Or contact us through our website www.pullnotpush.co.uk

Without YOUR interaction in this way, this would be just another dust collector. Helpful, unused, unloved.

I do not want to be the harbinger of doom but by not using this book the way it was intended could be the biggest loss your business could sustain. You've bought this book for a reason, right? I'm endeavoring to offer salvation to your business not contribute to its undoing.

After all, you could have the most brilliant business idea, the greatest invention or brightest product but if you cannot translate that into sales, it will be lost and left in the business cemetery, like many bright and brilliant ideas that have gone before.

So pencils at the ready folks!!!

Here we go……

Make it stick!

Chapter 1

Every Entrepreneur needs this book!!

CALLING ALL ENTREPRENUERS

Write your reflections and ideas here!

You have brains in your head. You have feet in your shoes. You can steer yourself, any direction you choose. – *Dr. Seuss*

I've seen how my Pull NOT Push, 1to1 and Corporate sales coaching has helped many entrepreneurs succeed in their ventures. I am also aware that every emerging business cannot afford my business coaching or training day rates (even if they are way below market rate). Plus there is only one of me. Which is why I wrote this book!

The great thing is that every budding entrepreneur with a great business idea can afford this brilliant book. Every entrepreneur needs the tools found in this book to be able to take their idea to market….. Without those tools, the best business idea in the history of all time will remain just that. AN IDEA!

And like my wise old Grandmother used to say….. "Well… you know what thought did!"

PEGGY MAY, MY WISE GRANDMOTHER

Write your reflections and ideas here!

You must either modify your dreams or magnify your skills. —
Jim Rohn

Even in the early days of securing funding 'selling' yourself and your business is essential.

My experience, however, is that it is very rare to find an Entrepreneur who is a slick salesperson or marketer. Well guess what? Now you don't have to be!!!

Simply follow the steps in this book and you will never have to be! You can just be yourself and the sales process will happen.

The characteristics that are shared by great Entrepreneurs AND great Salespeople are resilience and a high level of activity. You will still need this....

Resilience is just the mental strength to continue in adversity...you can build up resilience by just using the rationale that all success is a numbers game.

Resilience + Activity = Success

Doing the right thing, in the right way, over and over again can only lead one way...TO SUCCESS!

Write your reflections and ideas here!

Even if you are on the right track, You'll get run over if you just sit there. – *Will Rogers*

Chapter 2

Introduction

Don't skip this....understanding the motivation of your inspiration is essential!

And so it begins...for someone with a scatter brain, dyslexia, a diminished attention span and impulse control issues, writing a book is not the easiest of tasks. But I have learned over time and ENDLESS mistakes that having a process, a skeleton or strong framework to maximise the effectiveness of a well woven spell of wit and charm, is always the most effective way to not look like a complete crazy woman!

History has proven out that brilliance and breakthrough comes from unconventional thought. I am not sure that I would consider myself a brilliant brain, but my "disabilities" have gifted me the ability to find solutions through linking completely separate ideas and bringing them together to find a way that works for me...I have used these seemingly random and unconnected ideas to make an enthusiastic and empathic communicator into a highly effective selling machine. Now I want to share them with the world....with you.

Write your reflections and ideas here!

The great accomplishments of man have resulted from the transmission of ideas of enthusiasm. – *Thomas J. Watson*

THANK YOU

So the very first thing I want to do is THANK YOU for investing in this collection of selling ideology and personal rantings. I hope you find inspiration in the pages, I would love to hear your thoughts and reflections, successes, breakthroughs, failures and vow to personally answer all your questions on my website www.pullnotpush.co.uk. Feel free to link up with me on any of the social media sites.

Aaaaaahhhh... The joy of joined up online media. I am still a beginner at this, but I am learning and growing by the day, the elixir of life!

We are all beginners at anything new; I want to assure you that there are no stupid questions, so ask away. With this book you also buy my guidance during your early days while working these new methods.

If you feel that you need more guidance than a simple question will give you, then enroll on one of my workshops or access my personal coaching package via the website.

Write your reflections and ideas here!

It is not the strongest of the species that survive, nor the most intelligent, but the one most responsive to change. – *Charles Darwin*

The second thing I would like to do is to walk you through my motivation for writing this book and what I want to achieve.

I find that people are so busy trying to fathom what your motivation is that it interferes with any message that you may wish to deliver. You know.... that inner voice that shouts louder in this cynical world, the one that is internally screaming "yeah, yeah, okay, what does she really want?" It happens every time someone receives a cold call from anyone outside of their inner circle or remit (that'll be us, sales people!) I have found that if you're utterly honest about your motivation, you ARE polite and offer an alternative, enlighten them of your infinite worth in enabling THEIR work or career (if you don't have this you need to re-evaluate how you are marketing and what your selling strategy is!).

If you give people a valid reason, I guarantee, they will always be willing to give time and attention to a selling opportunity.

The bottom line is: You can stop people's objections and allow them to stop their distracting inner voices by just playing honest broker. Lay it on the line. Be clear.

Try it!

It breaks down barriers and creates a more personal engagement.

Write your reflections and ideas here!

The golden rule for every business man is this: Put yourself in your customer's place. – *Orison Swett Marden*

WHAT'S MY MOTIVATION?

So here it is….. My motivation.

I have a sales consultancy which helps SME's (Small to medium sized enterprises) and entrepreneurs I admire. Ones with good values and a vision of a life which makes a difference. I have found a way to help those who ask for my help in achieving their dreams, both personal and professional.

Entrepreneurs are The Innovators! The Dreamers! Those who dared to risk it all and start a business, buy a franchise, invent something marketable, find a solution or back an idea either emotionally or financially.

The Entrepreneur is not your average Joe. They are aspiring mothers, fathers, neighbours. Realising their dream. They are the opportunist who yearns for balance in establishing their enterprise whilst making a good living and supporting their family.

Write your reflections and ideas here!

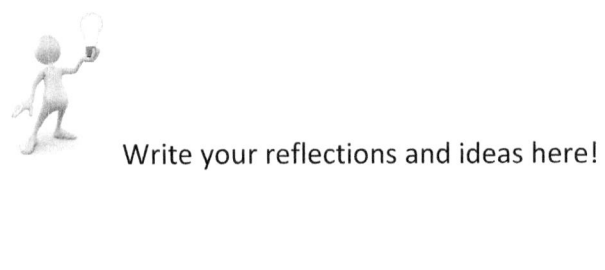

To win without risk is to triumph without glory. — *Pierre Corneille*

Pioneers of ingenuity, the Entrepreneur, will find and create different ways to enhance their fortunes and the fortunes of others.

That's where I come in; I cannot reach everyone, my time is limited. As a coach, I require a balanced life and there is only ONLY of one me. We return again to my motivation in writing this book, by replicating my methods in an easily digestible format, the problem is solved!

I have always said that it is all very well being brilliant at what you do; BUT, if you cannot find a way to replicate your brilliance, then you have a limited resource and you cannot build an empire on that! So…..here is my effort to replicate success for those people willing to seek their own solution.

This is also a perfect way for me to feed my passion. My key motivator is enabling the fortunes of others in whatever form I can. TADAH! Exposure to thousands of people I will never meet! The self-satisfaction of a job well done and a generous act that should keep the universe happy and working in my favour.

After a long career in collecting skills and experience, I have finally realised that the thing that turns me on most Is not money, although it brings me freedom and good times, it's turning around the fortunes of others, by giving them tools to achieve their dreams. Just having faith in someone allows them to flourish; I am an unstoppable nurturer!

Write your reflections and ideas here!

A successful man is one who can lay a firm foundation with the bricks others have thrown at him. – *David Brinkley*

I know it is said that whatever you chase will elude you happiness.... Money.... Power?

I HAVE A DREAM!

What I have found is that if you provide love, kindness and good fortune to others in an unselfish way, the universe provides more luck, love and privilege than you can imagine. Of course, you have to be eternally alert for the opportunities that present and you have to be clear that these tools are designed to be a giant opportunity trawling net.

Write your reflections and ideas here!

People are best convinced by things they themselves discover. – *Ben Franklin*

Now, this isn't supposed to be a preachy, hokey book... I hate those things!! I don't think you can have the stance of believing in the potential of every person without sounding a bit new age and flakey; or maybe that's just my prejudice against all things that take the power and influence over people's personal circumstance from them. If I have proved anything in my life it's that resilience and determination in the face of adversity, is the thing that makes you a remarkable human being. I have also proved that if you believe that you are truly worthy of success, then you will be.

What I have is an appetite to achieve..... I would like to hope that this little pocket book will be exactly that, a constant companion and friend to the owner. I hope that you can use my knowledge that has been proved out on many stages during my 25 years of being at the coal face of business development, to your benefit. I would like you to make this YOURS. Make it scruffy with constant use and writing in the margins (I have created extra space on every other page, so you can blend my ideas and processes with yours). I would like to think that the little gems in this book will be well merged seamlessly into your own processes and strategies that it brings you luck and the Ansell Magic I have been able to conjure.

So....my remarkable friend....my assumption is that if you have spent your hard earned money on this little book, then you are due some good fortune.

Write your reflections and ideas here!

I don't pay good wages because I have a lot of money; I have a lot of money because I pay good wages. – *Robert Bosch*

Keep positive. Keep those engines pumping. Apply my tools to your trade. I guarantee that people WILL listen to you. They will open their doors and wallets to you in a way that you have not experienced so far. Mainly because you have taken the lead in a way they have not experienced before.

Write your reflections and ideas here!

Opportunity is missed by most people because it is dressed in overalls and looks like work. – *Thomas Edison*

Chapter 3
My inspiration

I guess my inspiration has come from 4 major sources in my years.

The first is from my emerging from a modest working class background which fueled a need to create my own wealth and financially independence. Just like Vivien Leigh clutching the soil of Tara and vowing never to be hungry again, a girl from a family that just about gets by, learns to yearn for better things.

To be a working woman, mother, sportsperson and basically "have it all", I have always needed to find smart employment options, to accelerate my income, to have the ability to create freedom, flexibility and actually LIVE this life to the fullest.

I found very early on that the people with the least qualifications, those who got paid the most were on the cutting edge of selling. Remembering that I left school in the early 80's, working class kids didnt go to university. Instead, we had to get out there and earn a living. University was a middle or upper class luxury. It was also a time when we were launched into a world full of YUPPIES. Those young, upwardly mobile people, living the dream of anything is possible.

Write your reflections and ideas here!

Everyone is a genius. But if you judge a fish by its ability to climb a tree, it will spend its whole life believing it is stupid – *Einstein*

In order to succeed, I knew early on that I needed to learn the game from the best. I then had to wrestle the acquired knowledge into a palatable form for my sensitive self.

As time went on, I managed to position myself promoting services that not only made me serious money, but ones i could align with my altruistic tendencies.

First I worked in property, then onto financial services, sucking up knowledge and reworking old formats to my greater success.

After I took a break to make little people; I needed to find a high growth, cash rich, low start up cost industry, that was based around people and was fundamentally flawed...I found recruitment which led to my second great influencers.

I found a couple of American recruiting geniuses. One of these was Steve Finkle. An extraordinary non salesman with dubious facial hair, who though his books and videos bought me an understanding of Socratic selling and training techniques, RECIPROCITY (a word I still cannot spell or say! Thank the heavens for autocorrect).

Tony Byrne, another American recruitment guru (I wish I could carry those red braces off like he did) with his fantastic lessons on client control and positioning.

Write your reflections and ideas here!

Do or do not. There is no try. – *Yoda*

I urge you to seek out both of these brilliant selling minds to add to your skills library. I have seen their techniques work…. I believe they work in any industry if you are free thinking and open minded enough to embrace the concepts they convey.

Most of all, my techniques have been gifted to me from a surprisingly and unlikely place, that turned out to be the best EVER sales training in history!!

"What was this revelation?" I hear you ask. It was a person centered counselling course that I took when working towards becoming a foster carer 20 years ago.

WHAAAT?!?!?!

What? I hear you gasp. Your internal voice is not reassuring you that you have wasted your time and money.

NO! WAIT! HEAR ME OUT!

Whilst all the do-gooding, caring, healing types were learning about creating safe spaces for their future

clients to put all their experiences, traumas and reflections into, to make sense of their emotions, reactions and future paths.

Write your reflections and ideas here!

Your most unhappy customers are your greatest source of learning. –
Bill Gates

My commercial mind was fathoming the dynamic applications of this process for financial gain. I guess once a capitalist, always a capitalist!

What is she talking about? I hear your inner voice quizzing.

STICK WITH ME!

Ask yourself, how often do I get to share my professional pride, passions and needs?

How many people actually care enough to ASK you what your professional challenges and goals are?

How many people outside of our closest friends and allies actually take the time to find out what is troubling you during your working day?

I am not saying you have to be an agony aunt!

Far from it.

There couldn't be anything duller than listening to someone bitching about the office politics BUT finding out about the restraints and barriers to decision makers achieving their business targets.

Write your reflections and ideas here!

Leadership is doing what is right when no one is watching. – *George Van Valkenburg*

I cannot express enough how essential it is to find a way for your product or service to fit with your customer OR obtain information on how you can increase the business reason or motivation to buy. We can make assumptions about how your target market buy your offering and what makes them motivated to buy. The problem is we all know how dangerous assumptions are.

The only way you can really understand this is to draw it out of your customer and listen for THEIR agenda and work with them to bring about a happy transaction for all parties.

"That's great but how do we do that?" I hear you say.

We use the techniques I learned in my person centered counselling.

   a. You learn how to create a safe space to allow someone to speak and talk about their needs
   b. You understand and practice active listening
   c. You offer up probing and open questions
   d. You reflect the information back, learning to understand themes

All will become clear as we continue. There are examples of what this actually looks like in the two case studies in this book. There will be more on the website as it develops.

Just engaging and learning to listen to your customers is VERY powerful stuff!

Write your reflections and ideas here!

In the business world, everyone is paid in two coins: cash and experience. Take the experience first; the cash will come later. – *Harold Geneen*

It is disarming and highly charming. When you find the needs and the motivation in them, people will COMPLETELY buy into YOU. Then will find yourself having a meaningful business discussions INSTEAD of barking at them about how great your product is.

At the end of the day 'people buy people!' They buy service and they buy solutions. BUT they buy people first.

Using these techniques to reason your way into a sale changes everything for all parties involved and everyone wins.

Write your reflections and ideas here!

Those who say it can not be done, should not interrupt those doing it.
– *Chinese Proverb*

Chapter 4
Evolution – Past mistake and future solutions

Do you like to be "sold" to? The chances are that the answer is "No!" How does it make you feel?

Did you feel under pressure? Awkward? Like you are being barked at by the town crier? Manipulated? Bamboozled? Not able to think?

Can you think of a time when you have enjoyed being sold to? Actually, it is more likely that you enjoyed buying something and did not even realise you were being sold to. It takes a clever salesperson to who asked you what you wanted and needed. Then followed it up with a great solution that catered for both agendas and you probably got a great price too!

I have been through countless hours of sales training to find they have elements of interest and brilliant hints and tips. I guess the old adage that we only put into practice 10% of any training we undertake would be right in this context.

Write your reflections and ideas here!

Whatever the mind of man can conceive and believe, it can achieve. Thoughts are things! And powerful things at that, when mixed with definiteness of purpose, and burning desire, can be translated into riches. — *Napoleon Hill*

What I have seen from previous sales training and general sales tactics is that they are deeply entrenched in Pushy, "clever" tricks and ruses, macho posturing, glib retorts, smart answers and contrived practices to get the delegates to get one up on their potential customers.

Although there may be well worn ways to counter objections from experts embedded in that training, people do not like to feel "played" or "outsmarted". In reality, I feel that the things that work are: Being authentic, not creating an adversarial culture, understanding your worth and the commercial advantages of whatever it is that you are selling. Actively listening to the needs and wants of your customers, THEN delivering what you agree.

Write your reflections and ideas here!

The absolute fundamental aim is to make money out of satisfying customers. *– John Egan*

It is time as a business development/entrepreneur that you need to STOP pushing your needs. Listen to their needs/ agenda and start playing to your audience!

How do you do this? The great thing about entrepreneurs is that are completely passionate about the product or service they've creating their business around!

The pitfall of this enthusiasm and unerring belief is that some entrepreneurs forget to ascertain the appetite of the market. They also fail to identify who their target audience is.

It is essential to understand the needs and wants of your target market and how your product or service compares and competes with similar offerings.

Ask yourself what are the unique selling points of your business offering, how does is meet your customers' needs and what problems is it solving?

Knowledge of competing products and obtaining an objective view, along with closer alignment with your customer needs can be done with this system.

Understanding these things will make your marketing and pitching far easier and more effective.

How do you achieve this? Just ask them!

I will show you in the next few chapters exactly how this is done.

Write your reflections and ideas here!

If you would like to know the value of money, try to borrow some. –
Benjamin Franklin

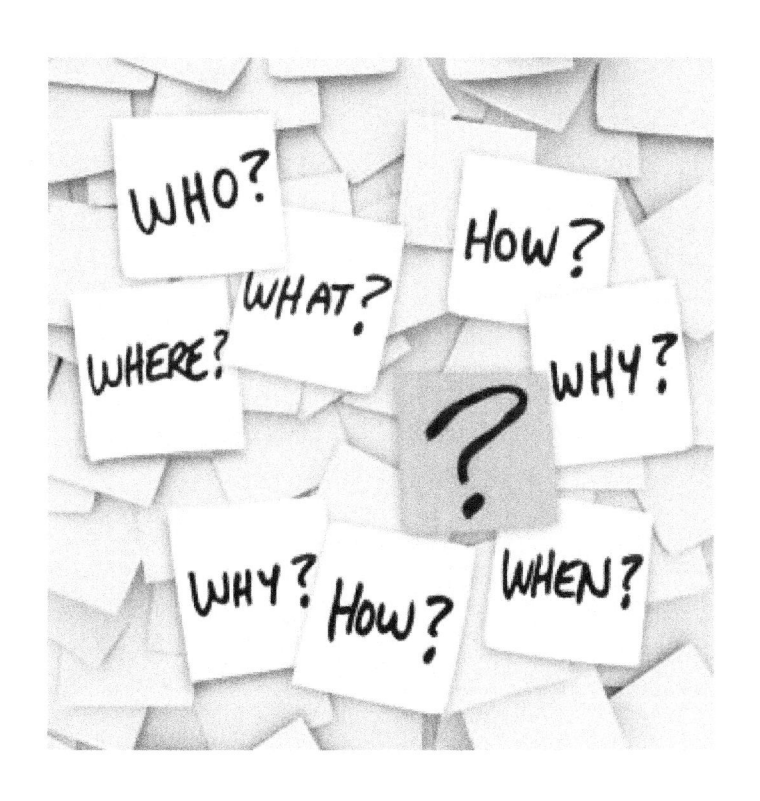

KNOW YOUR CUSTOMER

Write your reflections and ideas here!

If it really was a no–brainer to make it on your own in business there'd be millions of no–brained, harebrained, and otherwise dubiously brained individuals quitting their day jobs and hanging out their own shingles. Nobody would be left to round out the workforce and execute the business plan. — *Bill Rancic*

Chapter 5

Marketing AND Sales.....

Where does it all go wrong?

There is a great commonness to the entrepreneurs belief that "If you build it, they will come" Just like that great film, Field of dreams with Kevin Costner.

They feel that if they design/create/build their unique product, spend a fortune on the marketing, look, feel and tone. Buy a great website, packaging, then people will somehow just find your product, understand it and be motivated to use their hard earned money to buy it.

The problem is that there are thousands of brilliant products and services created by passionate potential entrepreneurs every year that never get off the ground.

Why is this?

The simple answer is that, for the most part you cannot usually be successful by passively marketing your offering. You have to identify who your customer is, where they are and how are you going to reach them.

Write your reflections and ideas here!

Winners take time to relish their work, knowing that scaling the mountain is what makes the view from the top so exhilarating. – *Denis Waitley*

This is the point that selling comes into play. Whoever you are trying to engage, it helps and is essential to have the right look, feel marketing and to understand your product but nothing can replace that active engagement that is sales.

You also need to understand that every buyer wants the impossible, which is a product which is inexpensive, high quality and they want it quickly.

In reality no one gets all three but in the words of the great Meatloaf, "Two out of three ain't bad".

If something is high quality and inexpensive, it's highly unlikely you will receive it quickly…. if it's cheap and quick then it is unlikely to be high quality…. and if high quality and fast… is going to be expensive!

What you need to understand is which combination of the two are you? This will help you position yourself in the market and how to market yourself most effectively. It will also help you position yourself in the pending sale.

You have to gauge your market, appetite for your product and your pricing to make sure you have a successful offering.

Write your reflections and ideas here!

Statistics suggest that when customers complain, business owners and managers ought to get excited about it. The complaining customer represents a huge opportunity for more business. – *Zig Ziglar*

This is not a marketing book and for the most part, entrepreneurs get all the marketing loveliness. The hard part is always the direct promotion to buyers of something that is loved and highly valued by the business builder.

The problem is that most entrepreneurs are so emotionally attached to their product that makes everything personal. It is at that point the internal resistance starts. The fear of selling which has a fear of rejection at its core.

It is difficult not to get emotionally attached to something you are passionate about. It is almost impossible to come across to your customers as authentic if you are not.

I cannot say do not be any of these things but what I do advise is that you stay open to reason and reality, be prepared to evolve in your approach or product to be successful. Keep your emotions in check…. Passion is essential but not as important as reality.

Find a way to mindfully reason your way through you selling process. Remember it is not personal and whilst you have to be present and attentive to every sale, there really is truth and success in understanding that it's just a numbers game.

Be utterly determined but also make sure you seek out the right advice to keep you on track and keep you selling.

Write your reflections and ideas here!

The only place success comes before work is in the dictionary. – *Vidal Sassoon*

That's where people like me and books like this come in handy. Helping you to find a way to connect with your audience, over and over again.

Write your reflections and ideas here!

The problem with the rat race is that even if you win, you're still a rat.
— *Lilly Tomlin*

Chapter 6
Pull NOT Push

What is this Pull NOT Push strategy? How and why does it work?

I like to think of some of the principals I have learned through Martial Arts, where the most effective way to floor an opponent is to go with the force they come at you with and allow them to vanquish themselves. Instead of being adversarial and matching blow to blow, you harness the power that gets thrown at you and go with it to achieve success….Pull NOT Push!

There is no resistance with a technique that goes with the natural flow of things and if you are working with the needs of your customer base you create minimal resistance. When you do hit resistance, the same techniques will move that resistance.

Write your reflections and ideas here!

The NBA is never just a business. It's always business. It's always personal. All good businesses are personal. The best businesses are very personal. – *Mark Cuban*

One thing you must remember. if a deal is going to go together it will go together. Trying to force any "sale" will rarely have the outcome you are looking for. FACT!

Very successful sales people NEVER rely on any one deal to carry them through. They create healthy pipelines to ensure their positioning is always one of strength and confidence. That their 'desperation' for any one sale does not influence the integrity of their business dealings. This is why they are successful and NOT because they have the gift of the gab or the luck of the Irish.

In fact, the only thing that makes a successful salesperson is hard work continually using the right processes consistently; Doing the right thing in the right way, over and over again. This whole idea that great salespeople are born and not made, for me, is a complete untruth.

Write your reflections and ideas here!

Your income is directly related to your philosophy, NOT the economy.
— Jim Rohn

There are those who are more determined and resilient, those who have a solid and unerring work ethic that keeps them moving forward with higher purpose. These people have all kinds of occupations and are actually the most likely to become entrepreneurs.

The theory behind Pull NOT Push is to utilise concepts that talking therapy counsellors of all types use. Create a "safe" space for a person to put all of their thoughts, needs , emotions, motivations, behaviours etc. into, so that a solution or way forward can be found.

How can this be of any use? All will be revealed!

In a Pull NOT Push selling process you would create an environment in which you can collect all of the relevant information through clever, predesigned questioning techniques or Socratic processes. 'Socratic' named after a Greek Teacher and Philosopher Socrates, he taught that you learn by asking questions of his students so they could fathom the answers through their own deduction. This is then used to collate all the relevant information in such a way that you and your customer are both on a journey to a sale together.

Write your reflections and ideas here!

Your time is precious, so don't waste it living someone else's life. – *Steve Jobs*

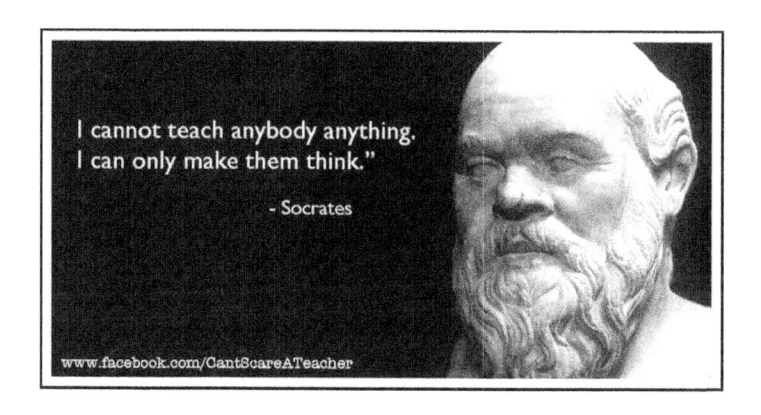

> I cannot teach anybody anything.
> I can only make them think."
>
> - Socrates

"What is so amazing about this?" I hear you say. Think about it! When the last time you were asked questions about what you want, or, what you need, or, what you want to achieve, or, what are your barriers to achieving this, in any context let alone in what you are trying to achieve in a workspace? This is a consultative process that is frequently used in Business to Business selling.

Write your reflections and ideas here!

A calm sea does not make a skilled sailor. – *Unknown*

The power of listening is the key dynamic here. When you are truly focused on the needs and wants of the other party, the relationship building process is in hyper drive.

TWO EARS ONE MOUTH!

This is an interesting dilemma! How can a selfishly motivated person be truly focused on the needs of others? I understand the skepticism; the key word here is focus! The less you cater to the needs of whoever the other person is, in whatever the situation you're in, the less likely you are to succeed. The simple truth is that if you live to serve, this becomes your salvation when it comes to "selling".

Write your reflections and ideas here!

Don't worry about people stealing your ideas. If your ideas are any good, you'll have to ram them down people's throats. – *Howard Aiken*

Knowing that understanding the needs and wants of other is the key to making your solution fit. If you assume what they are, or even worse do not even care what others want to achieve, then your efforts will always seem selfish, contrived and forceful.

I love Aesop's fable of the sun and the wind, if you are not familiar with it, here goes……

The North Wind boasted of great strength. The Sun argued that there was great power in gentleness.

"We shall have a contest," said the Sun.

Far below, a man traveled a winding road. He was wearing a warm winter coat.

"As a test of strength," said the Sun, "Let us see which of us can take the coat off of that man."

"It will be quite simple for me to force him to remove his coat," bragged the Wind.

The Wind blew so hard, the birds clung to the trees. The world was filled with dust and leaves. But the harder the wind blew down the road, the tighter the shivering man clung to his coat.

Then, the Sun came out from behind a cloud. Sun warmed the air and the frosty ground. The man on the road unbuttoned his coat.

The sun grew slowly brighter and brighter.

Soon the man felt so hot, he took off his coat and sat down in a shady spot.

Write your reflections and ideas here!

There is no security on the earth, there is only opportunity. – *General Douglas MacArthur*

"How did you do that?" said the Wind.

"It was easy," said the Sun, "I lit the day. Through gentleness I got my way."

THE NORTH WIND AND THE SUN

I took this brilliant and poignant fable as a clear sign that warming and charming a customer, giving them what makes them happy and comfortable is always a better way to sell than looking to force or outwit them.

I am constantly amused and surprised by those who ever considered that selling was ever going to be an adversarial game.

The whole idea is that you PULL people in and not PUSH them into submission or browbeat them with your will to win.

Write your reflections and ideas here!

Always forgive your enemies. Nothing annoys them more. – *Oscar Wilde*

Chapter 7
Designing strategies that work for you

Okay! Okay! You get the theory behind the strategy.

But how do you actually utilise the theory and create a system that is going to work for you?

You have to create a thought journey for your clients to guide them into recognising and embracing the benefits of what you are selling.

The process for creating a thought journey takes 6 simple steps.

1. Recognise the wide range of benefits of your offering to your current and future clients. You can do this by asking yourself what problems are your products solving and why are people buying/going to buy your product?

Write your reflections and ideas here!

To succeed... You need to find something to hold on to, something to motivate you, something to inspire you. – *Tony Dorsett*

2. Create a Socratic (learning through questioning) process. We do this by asking questions and Pulling the recognition of the customers own personal benefits through the purchasing of your product from the customer. This process isn't just a gimmick. The process of answering a question, requires a meaningful cerebral engagement. Conversely and to illustrate the point, if you tell or PUSH your opinion about the benefits, all a customer needs to do is passively hear what you are saying. If they still buy what you are selling, they were going to anyway and you haven't affected any change or influence.

PULLING = ACTIVE ENGAGEMENT

PUSHING = PASSIVE WITNESSING

The best way to do this is to format a "discovery document". This is a uniform questionnaire that forms the basis of your selling process.

3. Lastly and probably the most important step. Actively listen!

Write your reflections and ideas here!

To think creatively, we must be able to look afresh at what we normally take for granted. – *George Kneller*

'Definition of Active Listening is a communication technique used in counselling, training and conflict resolution, which requires the listener to feed back what they hear to the speaker, by way of restating or paraphrasing what they have heard in their own words, to confirm what they have heard and moreover, to confirm the understanding of both parties.' Wikipedia.

I could probably write a whole chapter on active listening. I run workshops specifically on this subject.

I recognised the power of this skill and its applications whilst training as a counsellor. As you mindfully ask all your questions, you have to attend and observe the responses to them. Without this, you will miss the "hot buttons" your customers will reveal to you.

Hot buttons are the keys to closing a sale. They reveal your customers ultimate motivations or reasons for buying. They are buttons you must identify so you can press them at the optimum moment.

Your reflection of these hot buttons back to the customer, maybe even probe deeper for extra recognition or for the effect of truly understanding their needs, will be the way you or make your point and a sale.

Write your reflections and ideas here!

Successful people are the ones who are breaking the rules. – *Seth Godin*

4. Summarise your Q&A session, highlighting the points discovered in the process. This process galvanises the buyer/seller relationship by showing a higher level of customer care and attention, which builds a huge amount of trust.

   I call this the sense checking part of the process, my waterproofing stage. You should sense check or waterproof your sale at all stages of your selling process, making sure that you are not taking your sale for granted. Certainly most business to business sales are conducted over a number of meetings, they usually have a higher cost to them and need to go through a procurement process with a number of sign offs or crucial decision making points. These are now common practice since the recession as there is now less margin for error. People are far more aware and cautious when making buying decisions. As any investment or buying decision can now have a catastrophic effect on the overall running and commerciality of the business.

5. Confirm that your customer wants to buy from you and your company. It is rare that anyone has an exclusively unique product or offering. If you have, then great, but it's more likely that you have a variation on a theme, or you have competitors.

Write your reflections and ideas here!

Yesterday's home runs don't win today's games. — *Babe Ruth*

People buy from people. At this stage you should have built a level of trust and understanding that is unparalleled in any buyers experience. It's time to test this. Be bold, but remain humble. You do not need the resistance of a personality clash to pull down a sale. It is better to assign the sale to someone else than to lose it down to a chemistry thing.

Most customers need to have a level of trust and reassurance when placing their order with you. They need to know that you will deliver according to your promises. This could be down to size, establishment, personalities, communication or financial security. You have to find out what these often hidden objections are and overcome them.

6. The Close. A close doesn't need to be a dramatic finish! In this processes case it is a simple, final and basic closing question.

Question format

You have told me that you need ABC and your motivation to buy is 123 and that your budget or projected spend is XYZ....If we can do ABC, satisfy 123 within XYZ, are you going to be doing business with me?

At this stage, if you have completed all steps with due care, the buyer will have little room to maneuver and will be completely willing and happy to give you a big fat **YES!**

Write your reflections and ideas here!

To think is easy. To act is difficult. To act as one thinks is the most difficult. — *Johann Wolfgang Von Goeth*

All that follows are the operational steps to make that happen and those need to be understood. This is not the time to start working against the customer and the collaborative mode of the interaction so far. You do not lose control of the sale by moving at someone else's pace that only happens when you lack understanding of internal or external processes.

Write your reflections and ideas here!

Surviving a failure gives you more self-confidence. Failures are great learning tools... but they must be kept to a minimum. – *Jeffrey Immelt*

Chapter 8
Examples to demonstrate

The way you learn will hugely affect the way you take on these methods. I am a kinesthetic learner, for the most part I learn and understand new concepts by doing and experiencing examples of any new learning. This is why I feel that having real life case studies is a good way to show off new methods and their range of applications.

So here we have two very different examples of my coaching with very different businesses and the systems we created to successfully drive their businesses forward.

Case study 1 - The Inventory Franchisee

Donna is a lettings specialist of 15 years who decided to invest a significant amount of money in a high-tech inventory franchise but had stalled so badly in her business development activity to the point that she was about to give up on her business. Her reaction to the thought of picking up the phone or selling her services was almost phobic.

Write your reflections and ideas here!

Please think about your legacy, because you're writing it every day. – *Gary Vaynerchuck*

Donna had every reason to be negatively and positively motivated to engage with her selling responsibilities, but still could not face prospecting.

It was clear she needed to turn this whole reaction on its head by changing her perception of her service and by creating a Socratic, Pull NOT Push selling process.

After sitting down and understanding how management companies and landlords fulfil this part of their process, we decided that her service was actually very reasonable, easily accessible, quick and efficient, a truly excellent product which she believed in completely. Of course she did! I hear you scream. What kind of idiot invests thousands of their own money in something they do not fully and completely commit to?

All admirable qualities, but no matter how brilliant the product Donna couldn't bring herself to share this great product with the world. Even though she was lacking the income she desperately needed, she was completely disabled and disarmed when it came to taking her fabulous service to market.

Picking up the phone to Lettings Agents and Management Companies was a complete no-no for her. The mere thought of cold calling terrified her.

Write your reflections and ideas here!

The man who will use his skill and constructive imagination to see how much he can give for a dollar, instead of how little he can give for a dollar, is bound to succeed. – *Henry Ford*

Like any sales function, it's great to have an awesome offering, fabulous marketing materials, a great website but if you can't bring yourself to engage with your potential customers, then you are dead in the water.

Most people struggle with "selling", they talk themselves out of their ability to achieve sales and the worth of their product to potential customers. They get so absorbed in what they want to achieve by selling the product, that they lose sight of the benefits to the customer. They could actually be doing a huge favour by reaching out to the potential client armed with knowledge of their goods and services. They mistake their position in this interaction and think it in some way selfish or adversarial. One of the first things they have to change is their POSITIONING in this transaction.

The Pull NOT Push methodology requires the salesperson to tap into the agenda of their target; To truly understand why a business leader would be motivated to spend their overstretched, valuable time to meet with them and change the way they fulfil this part of their business service when it seems to be running perfectly well without it.

Write your reflections and ideas here!

The true entrepreneur is a doer, not a dreamer. – *Unknown*

With some digging and evaluating the lettings business, how it operates, what drives it and what the business structure tends to look like, we not only understood what our approach might be but also, how we could save their business thousands of pounds a month by outsourcing this part of the letting process.

It seems that, for the most part, lettings companies charged their lettings agents, who are predominantly sales type personalities, this detailed fairly boring part of the job, is not a great fit with these types of personalities. Furthermore, sales type personalities are better implemented elsewhere, unless they are trying to avoid their business development responsibilities, of course.

We found out that for Donna to complete the inventory and to have it uploaded, published and distributed, it took her under 2 hours. Meaning that she could complete up to 5 inventories a day without breaking a sweat. For the standard lettings agent, they could realistically only complete 2 a day.

Write your reflections and ideas here!

I feel that luck is preparation meeting opportunity. – *Oprah Winfrey*

I asked the question "If the letting agent had those 2 inventories outsourced, What else could they easily achieve instead of spending the day on those?" We decided that spending that time developing new tenants and landlords, in a day they could easily get one new tenant and one new landlord on board. This would provide and initial income of around £1500 per day. We also discovered that the average letting agent would do 4 inventories week, taking up 2 days of their working week.

Walking Donna through the value of her offering and what might motivate her customers to want to use her service, I discovered that on using her service which cost £150, she could create 20 times that amount for her client!

I asked Donna "If you had to call a potential customer to tell them that she could make their business an extra £3000 a week for an outlay of a tenth of that amount, how easy would that be?"

While we worked through this analysis of the lettings business model, all the lights started to switch on for Donna, her face became more and more lit up. With this one process Donna was able to see her prospecting calls in a completely different light.

Write your reflections and ideas here!

The winners in life think constantly in terms of I can, I will, and I am. Losers, on the other hand, concentrate their waking thoughts on what they should have or would have done, or what they can't do. – *Dennis Waitley*

Instead of calling up her customers trying to motivate them into buying her service over their in-house system which were working perfectly well up until now, she was calling her customers to make them an extra £3000 a week!

You can imagine what a different call that would feel like and how excited she became at the thought of helping all those businesses out there, rather than pushing her wares.

So with that mental and emotional barrier to selling well and truly out of the way, we embarked on creating a Pull NOT Push proforma to give body, strength, direction and substance to her business development call.

We decided to create two Pull NOT Push questionnaires, one for the decision maker and one for a Gatekeeper or someone in the business that answered the phone who wasn't a decision maker. Both conversations are equally important, although the decision maker is the one that writes the cheques, you can create excellent advocates out of a gatekeeper.

Of course we all know that we could be the best salesman with the best pitch, but if you're not talking to the person who can write the cheque, you may as well be whistling into the wind.

Write your reflections and ideas here!

The successful man is the one who finds out what is the matter with his business before his competitors do. – *Roy L. Smith*

Donna's Gatekeeper Questionnaire

Make sure you have a great introduction, engaging and warm, always ask for their help and pause while they agree to help. Let them know what you are asking for and what it would mean to you. Remember always be the Honest Broker!

1. Confirm basic information
2. Who is the decision maker
3. How do you feel is the best way to engage them
4. In your opinion, when it comes to inventory creation, what do you think the perfect scenario is? Feel free to use a softener….If you were the inventory fairy for the day and could create a perfect scenario for your inventory provision, what would that look like? (is the one that Donna identified with)

Make sure you follow up with a really friendly thank you and reward them in some way for their help. Turn your gatekeeper into a cheerleader, you will be surprised how much of a difference it makes to your success in reaching and engaging the decision maker.

Write your reflections and ideas here!

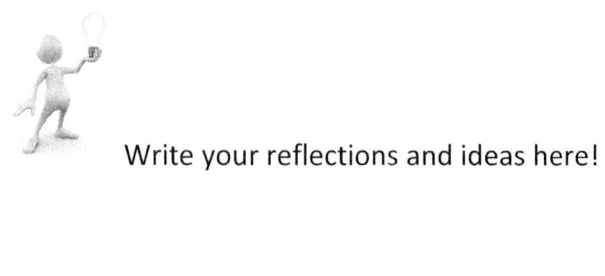

A man should never neglect his family for business. – *Walt Disney*

Donna's Decision maker Questionnaire

Again, introduce yourself and what you hope to achieve with your call, how long it will take and whether its a good time to talk.

Big tip! Make sure you pay reverence to your question and once you ask, just stay quiet and allow your decision maker to answer fully.

1. Confirm information and status
2. How do you currently fulfil your inventory requirement/function
3. What would be your perfect scenario (feel free to use softeners)
4. What would motivate you to move to your perfect scenario?

Follow up with a close, which is very simply

5. when can I come and see you?

Keeping this simple and listening to the answers and ideas from both gatekeepers and decision makers transformed the conversations that Donna was having. From awkward and hesitant calls to warm friendly, progressive and inclusive business conversations. These have enabled Donna to grow along with her contracts.

> Keep
> It
> Simple (and)
> Straighforward

Write your reflections and ideas here!

Live daringly, boldly, fearlessly. Taste the relish to be found in competition – in having put forth the best within you. – *Henry J. Kaiser*

Let me just say at this point, Donna's reaction and behaviours around her business development responsibilities was VERY typical. A pattern that I have seen time and time again and probably will repeated infinitem.

Write your reflections and ideas here!

We generate fears while we sit. We over come them by action. Fear is natures way of warning us to get busy. – *Dr. Henry Link*

Case Study 2 - Age Advisory Company

This is an example from my most favourite consultancy contract for a number of reasons, the people, the groundbreaking business concept, the blue chip target market made this an irresistible business development opportunity for me.

The fact that I would be able to personally prove out my methods by being responsible for the delivery as well as the strategy and processes only increased the attractiveness of the contract.

I was engaged by two fabulous Australian brothers; One had written a brilliantly useful and helpful handbook on aging positively and the other had created an online platform designed for corporations which positively supported their aging workforce. A fascinating fact is that 50% of the working population would be over 50 by the year 2020 and that 1 in 5 workers in the UK had carer responsibilities. The financial impact on these corporations would, without question, be astronomical in the years to come.

Write your reflections and ideas here!

A business has to be involving, it has to be fun, and it has to exercise your creative instincts. – *Richard Branson*

This was a completely new product with no competitors and the business development aim was to get in front of as many influential, key decision makers in as many blue chip companies as possible. The added problem, to cap all problems...NO ONE had even thought about creating a budget for a problem they didn't even know they had. This meant that any sale was going to, not only be a huge education project but it would also mean that we would need to convince the purse string holders that they needed to find more money in order to save themselves time and lots of money in the future.

As part of my brief I designed this proforma to use while opening doors and starting negotiations to get big corporates to buy a completely untested new virtual product.

How did we use this?

  A. We created a list of the companies and the contacts within those companies who had an interest in supporting the workforce and who would have influence on employee benefits budgets.

It was designed to discover and uncover the

Write your reflections and ideas here!

Whether you think you can or whether you think you can't, you're right! – *Henry Ford*

B. knowledge, provision and most importantly gaps in the corporate support for an ageing population. We then used this socratic guide to structure meaningful conversations with key stakeholders and book a more significant meeting to educate on shortfall of provision, commercial impact of this shortfall and to link into the decision making structure to the final close.
C. The first part of the form was simply designed to map out the client contact information that we needed to identify the sales targets and decision making responsibility of each contact, also to widen our knowledge of the hierarchy and how we could interact with them via their channels.

Please see the notes in each section in the questionnaire to understand the reasons why each section was created.

Write your reflections and ideas here!

Every accomplishment starts with a decision to try. – *Unknown*

UNDERSTANDING WHY EACH QUESTION WAS CREATED AND HOW YOU CAN USE IT IS AN INCREDIBLY INSIGHTFUL WAY TO START TO CREATE YOUR OWN TEMPLATE

Company:	Contact:
Title:	Interest:
Telephone:	Email:

Groups/source: ENEI/EFC/BITC/Carers UK
Linkedin/our news feed/twitter
Other Networks/Groups?

Referred to: e.g. HR, FD, Diversity and Inclusion, Employee Bens, Carer Network?
Name:
Contact info:
Interest:
Name :
Contact info:
Interest: *collecting all this information in the first instance plays out the "flattering and effective, tell me about yourself, you are important to me" part of the process*

What do they know about our company?
Classic Pull NOT Push opening question!! This is designed to explore and expose. The saying Never assume anything is powerful here.

Key Challenges to business around Positive ageing/ageing workforce?
This question is designed to uncover ALL of the clients HOT BUTTONS....Follow up the answers to this question with a process of "that is really interesting", "what else?", "probing questions", "what else?" and never feel uncomfortable by asking the same question to gain a full understanding. Your diligence in this area will prove to be both endearing and intoxicating.

Where does our company fit?
Asking where they think you fit, rather than telling someone where you see yourself (for a traditional sales professional, this will be almost torturous!) will uncover the fast route to the initial sale and low hanging fruit. It also waterproofs the fact that this is their chance to get what they need and feel empowered and understood.

What budget has been defined for your provision & who are the Key Stakeholders?
This is designed to find out what spend has been allocated to "solve" their issues and who the decision makers and influencers are. It means that you will understand the provision you would need, your path to the sale and the people you need to engage on the way to closing the deal. It would also uncover how important and pressing the solution is and what shortfall there might be. It would

uncover, in this case, how much educating was required to increase budget to a reasonable level. With the products this company sold, they were trailblazing on an impending and unavoidable trend which has significant and mostly hidden financial impact.

Their Strategy for Ageing workforce
Again this is designed to understand and expose the needs of the client and give an opportunity to give great service by giving advice on how they could improve in the next meeting. Remember this is a fact finding exercise in a corporate selling process.

Seminar Offer? *This was the ultimate close in this process.*

While these seminars did not make any money (although many clients had budget and were willing to pay for seminars!) What this did do was commit the decision maker to work with you and created a high level of reciprocity.

This was a "give to get" way to educate the client on their undiscovered need and to gain further information to reinforce the concept and need for the company's products.

Creating a give to get is a way to show selflessness and a willingness to be of service. A complex free taster type of offering.

This is an example of a front line opening process that is essential for the effective and efficient running of a high level corporate sale. It was part of a larger selling strategy and process. This kind of process seems to be the manner of selling in a business to business or B2B environments.

This is one of the more complex sales processes I have worked with. The higher the ticket value, the more complex the process seems to work out.

The more simple selling processes I have encountered are in what is known in sales circles as B2C or Business to Consumer selling, like retail environments or direct sales strategies.

In complete contrast, Donna's sales process was very simple.

a. make phone contact
b. book a face to face closing meeting
c. deliver on customer needs

If you are in a simpler business with a lower ticket value then it is always simple.

There are full versions available in the Members Area of our website.

To become a member is free if you have completed one of the Pull NOT Push workshops or personal coaching sessions.

There are more examples of questionnaires and case studies on the website www.pullnotpush.co.uk

Write your reflections and ideas here!

Imagination is everything. It is the preview of life's coming attractions.
— *Albert Einstein*

Chapter 9
Identifying your selling process

Every sector, industry or product type will have its own selling process, whether yours is a business to consumer sale or a business to business sale. This process has to be understood and a considered process identified so that you can accurately create and project your pipelines.

Creating an adequate pipeline for sustained business growth is an essential for success.

It means that you can sense check and keep control of a sale, accurately predict outcomes, as well as make adjustments to sales activity and performance.

Performance management is an essential part of any successful selling function and without first identifying the process you cannot hope to manage the performance or business development.

Below is an example of a fairly complex, high ticket business to business sales process from one of my former consultancies.

The Age Advisory Company defined sales process Overview
1. Identify and engage
2. Meetings and Negotiations
3. Close, Roll out and operations
4. Account management and renewal

Write your reflections and ideas here!

One finds limits by pushing them. – *Herbert Simon*

Break down

1. Identify and engage
a. Identify company
b. Identify decision maker
c. Engage via email/Linkedin
d. Initial call

2. Meetings and Negotiations

Stage	Agenda	Goal	Tools
1st Meet	Intro/fact find/portal demo/way forward/uncover current challenges	Build rapport, understanding and book 2nd meeting	Brochure Fact find template (need and education)/agenda lay out/confirmation email/ thank you email/initial proposal template
2nd Meet	Present initial proposal/uncover objections/understand hot spots/schedule seminars	Identify key stake holders/decision makers Book seminars	2nd Fact find (objections and challenges) PP Presentation/initial proposal/admin emails
Seminars	Delivery/engagement Management Information collection	Deliver and engage employees and DM's Book 3rd Meeting	Seminar schedules PP doc and formats MI collection/feed

			back systems Promotional materials Admin emails
3rd Meet	Key stake holder engagement Delivery of all Management info collected in presentation. Stake holder fact find	Engagement of all stakeholders Pre-close proposal and Business case Book 4th meeting	Brochures Stake holder fact find Management information document Admin emails
4th Meet	Presenting Business case uncover objections or issues	Delivery of business case Uncover final objections Pre-close on hand shake Book 5th meeting	Business case template Objections fact find Business case document Admin emails
5th Meet	Final presentation Q&A Handshake	Hand shake and book closing meeting	Final presentation template Objections template Presentation/final proposal hand out Admin emails
6th	Review and sign	Complete	Contracts

Meet		Paperwork Payment schedule	
Operational roll out	Rolling out / engagement/delivery	Agree on Schedule Book engagement programme	Roll out schedule Promotional material Admin emails

3. Close, Roll out and operations
a. Contracts
b. Operation planning and delivery
c. Promotional/engagement schedule

4. Account management and renewal
a. Set up account management agreement and contact
b. Set review schedules/meetings
c. management information reporting
d. Renewal process

It may seem a little arduous to formally identify and set out this process in such specific terms, smart people don't need to break things down to this level do we?

Actually, when you are breaking down any process to increase performance, any margin of improvement can be the game changer. It's not necessarily just the devil you will see in the detail but your saviour could also be hiding there!

Write your reflections and ideas here!

You must be the change you wish to see in the world. – *Mahatma Gandhi*

Chapter 10
The elements of success
The triangle

This parting section of the book is designed to give you some ultimate wisdoms that I have tried and tested throughout my business development career.

The following are absolute gems. Understanding these will give you added support and enhance your efforts.

Assume Nothing

I know this sounds very obvious and basic but the second you assume or allow yourself assumptive license then you are on a slippery slope to impending failure!

The best way to ensure this is to get others to look at your deals and ask probing questions about the likelihood or substance of the prospect and sense check it.

If you start to feel yourself guessing or assuming answers, you should realise that you need to go back to your client and gain control rather than assuming that you have it!

Nature abhors a vacuum

The art of selling is not about what you say or the gift of the gab but in understanding when to say nothing.

To use silence in a way that allows the process to be strong and effective.

How do you do this?

Simple! Ask a clearly defined, well thought out question and then **SHUT UP** and listen for the response.

Do not speak! Do not be afraid of uncomfortable silences. **Use them!**

Nature abhors a vacuum! The whole premise of Pull NOT Push depends on you creating an empty space to be filled by your customer, so please observe the space and hold it sacrosanct.

Positioning

I have learned that positioning and confidence is essential to someone in a selling role.

Know your worth! Be utterly convinced of your worth to your customer.

What do I mean by this? And why is this so important?

The first ever sale you make is to yourself. If you believe your worth, the worth of your product and its delivery then your "sale" or selling will come across as authentic.

Authenticity is essential! You cannot blag a sale unless the customer is desperate to buy. The only way blaggers sell is on price! Whilst keen pricing for your market is a key part of any sale, you cannot sell on price alone without devaluing your offering.

There are two kinds of salespeople in this world; weak price merchants and strong consultative salespeople who sell on value and quality.

This whole process is consultative. If you are still selling on price alone, this book will be wasted on you!

When you make any contact with a potential customer you cannot go cap in hand, no one buys from the needy.

It is widely understood that people will always listen to the most confident person in the room, the same is true of selling. Whether a customer is parting with a few pounds or a few hundred thousands pounds, they need to feel confidence in you and comfort that what they are buying will answer all their needs and wants.

An obvious statement? This is true, but I have delivered messages to many people at many levels and you would be surprised how obvious you need to be at times. Whilst I am not attempting to insult your intelligence, I am trying to make sure this one is delivered in the most complete way.

Getting your positioning right does not mean you strut around pigeon-like, full of false importance. It is about having absolute belief in your offering and its worth. At this point you need also to understand it's worth to your customer and how it caters to their needs.

These methods allow you to uncover this and in doing this, with the correct positioning, you will be able to maximise both your opportunity and your profitability.

Five Building blocks for success - Inspiration from the house of Steve Finkle

There are five building blocks that will make you a successful Business Developer in any industry!

1. Attitude and positioning

The right attitude carried through all that you do will mean that people respond to you in a positive way.

Understanding how important you can be to the success of your client companies will give you the gravitas and determination to educate people to our way, increasing your door-opening success.

2. Capacity for Hard Work

You will have all you need to, with the help of this book , to make you successful, all you need to do is apply it.

There is a straight line between what you put in and what you get out in business.
There has to be a willingness to consistently pay the price and the price is plain, old fashioned, hard work.

Of course the really successful people in any industry work smart but they also work hard.

3. Listening

Listening is an absolute essential for building any business and my methods dictate that you are a master listener. I don't mean just hearing what someone says; I mean actually attending the conversations you have to the fullest extent, giving you the ability to hear what people are really telling you and what they are not telling you.
This makes it possible to spot all the opportunities and leads that present themselves during any conversation and it makes people feel that you have their interests at heart which is immediately engaging and the core of what we are looking to achieve here - be an effective detective!

Listening is **hard work** if done properly!

4. Planning

Without planning your day can never be as productive as you would like. You come to work every day so make every day count.

It is reckoned that a person can be as much as five times more effective if they plan ahead. Think about it, five times more effective means five times more money!
Think about what your average day, week, month looks like and what time you should spend on essential tasks to make you function at your highest level. Design your planner to ensure every part of your day is calculated and planned out. It means that the second you do get an emergency task which must take priority, you can simply revert back to your plan rather than bumbling around trying to remember what you were supposed to be doing when you were rudely interrupted.

Any planner can be used to analyse your performance in retrospect, you cannot hide from the truths shown in a well utilised planner.
I am a massive advocate for planners for members of a sales team, it means that you can support them effectively. Sales people, notorious for their free spirited flare, indiscipline and dislike for management, however, will hate them! Explain the benefits in pounds, shillings and pence, they will convert (in the end).

5. Ethics

You must be prepared to work ethically, treating people with respect, honouring your commitments and confidentialities.
This will pay you huge dividends and create a sustainable and referrable business which will turn into an empire.
Treat everyone as you would wish to be treated, do the right thing by everyone. If you cannot conduct your business in an ethical way, rethink and find a new way because an unethical way will not build anything lasting or satisfying.

Triangles

In fact this triangulation can been seen and reflected in many areas of life and its functions.

I am fascinated by triangles and triangulation. Triangles are the strongest of all shapes and create the strongest of all structures. Look at all of the most fabulous structures in history, starting with the pyramids, enormous bridges, to the Eiffel Tower and to modern geodesic structures like the Gherkin. It's a personal geeky obsession to see shapes and patterns that make sense of this world. I thought I would share this simple and easily remembered pictorial representation to selling success. The fire triangle.

My final point is in part a a small homage to my beloved late father, 17 years a London fireman.

It occurred to me during a recent business development contract that the elements in the success of a sale were very similar to a formula I remembered about keeping a fire alive!

To keep a fire alive you need 3 things: Fuel + Oxygen + Heat = Fire

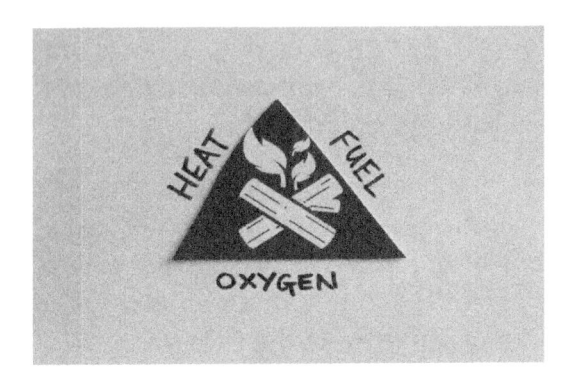

If you cut off any one of these things the fire instantly dies.

The same rings true about a business development process.

You need to have these three things:

Focus/strategy + Effort/activity + Control = Sale

Cut one of these things off and your business will die.

MY DAD

And finally.......
About the Author

Lisa Ansell is the brains and creator of Pull NOT Push. She is also a mother and grandmother.
With nearly 30 years business development delivery and consulting, coaching and sales training experience.
Lisa brilliantly but simply turns traditional thinking on its head to allow you to have inclusive and mindful business conversations with your customers.

This book is the culmination of over 30 years of sales knowledge and experience, many highs, achievements, as well as challenges and lessons. Lisa has worked at all levels, in all kinds of industries. The sector has never really mattered as you can easily pick up the relevant sector specific information by using these methods.

What people have said about Lisa as a Business Development Consultant/Coach

Lisa is a fantastic business development professional who has brought a wealth of experience, knowledge and enthusiasm to our new team. A natural leader who operates as efficiently and effectively at the broader strategic level as she does at the detailed tactical level. Lisa is a wonderful communicator and as far as engagement and relationship-building goes, is a force of nature. A first class sales and business development professional who we are very pleased to have on our team.

Chris Minnet, Managing director, Mercer Ageing Works

Lisa hit the ground running for us, communicating and integrating herself with our business and clients to understand their needs, pressures and methodologies in order to start raising awareness of the costly challenges (and opportunities) that an ageing workforce presents and then to help these organisations to move forward by developing and providing valued solutions that help them prepare for and manage their ageing workforce.

Lisa combines her razor sharp business development skills and experience with a personality that is great fun, generous, understanding and patient and always operates to the highest level of integrity.

I have been repeatedly impressed with the way Lisa helps me to get things done under moments of extreme pressure and I would not hesitate to recommend her.

Mike Minnet, Founder and MD of The Positive Ageing Company

Quite simply Lisa delivers. She knows how to get what the client wants and she makes it happen. Highly recommended.

Sue Cook, Owner COREcr & Brainbuzz

Lisa worked with us to develop and implement a direct sales process. I was very pleased with her professionalism and input. I am hoping to work with Lisa again to help further develop our process.

Elliot Smith, Managing Director Website design LTD

Lisa has literally saved me from giving up on my new business! I have always hated sales but somehow, she has turned it all round for me with her coaching and fun approach so that I'm no longer freaked out by making those dreaded sales calls, I'm actually enjoying them and having a bit of fun with it. Totally recommended for anyone like me who isn't one of those pushy sales people we all dislike!

I have spent many years doing sales in one form or another but truthfully, have always hated it. I went to great lengths to get into work that did not involve daily selling, as well as spending a lot of money investing in a franchise.

Great, I thought no more selling but as common sense would dictate, when you run your own business, there is always an amount of selling to do especially when you are offering a service.

I found myself almost paralysed when it came to selling my services and found anything and everything else I could do not to pick up the phone. Then Lisa happened!!!

At the most perfect time, Lisa offered me coaching that would make such a massive difference to my mindset on selling, I just had to say something about it.

It sounds extreme but she has taken all the fear out of selling for me, she has even made it fun for me, would you believe?

So, although selling is still not my favourite thing to do I'm just not scared of it anymore and happily pick up the phone and get cold calling. Fabulous lady!

Donna Turner, Property Franchise owner

More on the website

You're Invited!

Please get in touch

Thank you for taking the time to read my little book

Lisa Ansell

PS. If you tell the truth for long enough you are bound to get found out!

Chapter 13

What Next?

You've read the book and the foreword, taken it all in, have ploughed the internet for the T-shirt and have failed miserably to find one with my face and motto on it. I may well have missed a merchandising opportunity but I am good with that as the concept was a little too narcissistic.

If you have any simple questions to support you applying these principles to your own operation then drop me a line via the website and I guarantee I will reply.

If you need more complex support there are other options to get you fluent in the ways of Pull NOT Push. The first, being our brilliant half day workshops that take place around the country (see the website for details).

If you are not near to a workshop in the time you require it, there is always the personal coaching option. Simply drop me an email via the website requesting a time slot for your very own personal coaching session with me and we will use the allotted space to create a process that fits your needs exactly.

I look forward to hearing from you

Footnote

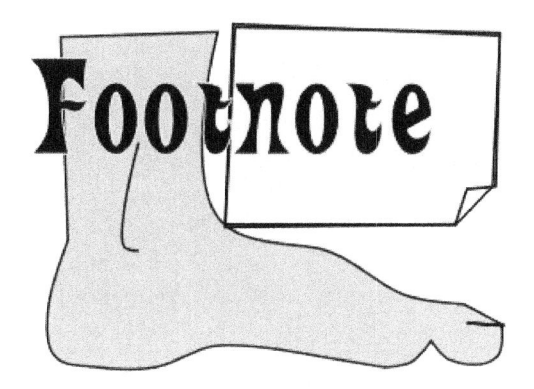

I always love to have the final word, in a perfect world we would always have the satisfaction of the last word…..

What I have as a final word is a way to make the world perfect…

RECIPROCITY

Definition: A situation in which two people or groups help each other by behaving in the same way or by giving each other similar advantages.

This is also the business ideal also…..

Live generously and you will be abundant.

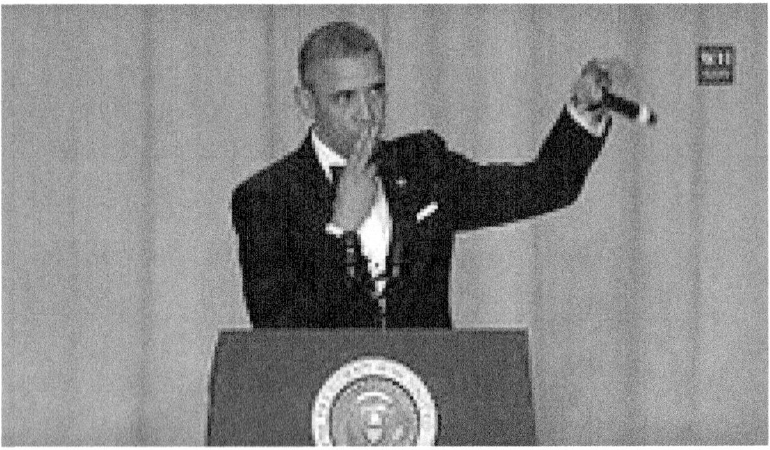

Printed in Great Britain
by Amazon